Copy

Dolores Dorantes

Copy

Translated by Robin Myers

Wave Books
Seattle & New York

Published by Wave Books

www.wavepoetry.com

Copyright © 2022 by Dolores Dorantes and Robin Myers

Wave Books titles are distributed to the trade by

Consortium Book Sales and Distribution

Phone: 800-283-3572 / SAN 631-760X

Library of Congress Cataloging-in-Publication Data

Names: Dorantes, Dolores, 1973– author. | Myers, Robin, 1987– translator.

Title: Copy / Dolores Dorantes ; translated by Robin Myers.

Other titles: Copia. English

Description: First edition. | Seattle : Wave Books, [2022]

Includes bibliographical references.

Identifiers: LCCN 2021043205 | ISBN 9781950268573 (hardcover)

ISBN 9781950268566 (paperback)

Subjects: LCGFT: Poetry.

Classification: LCC PQ7298.14.O64 C6713 2022

DDC 861/.64—dc23/eng/20211018

LC record available at https://lccn.loc.gov/2021043205

Designed by Crisis

Excerpt from *In the Presence of Absence* by

Mahmoud Darwish, translated by Sinan Antoon,

is reprinted with permission of Archipelago Books.

Printed in the United States of America

9 8 7 6 5 4 3 2 1

First Edition

Wave Books 099

This is I. This is he.

This is the miserable one, son of the miserable man and miserable woman. Son of your water and fire. I came from you, from nothingness, from one of your old poems, I came. I came from the imagination to return it to you and to carve your name, in stone like all the other poets of this wasteland. I asked a mule about its father and it said to me:

My uncle is a horse. Then it disappeared.

I asked a girl about her father. She became shy and she said: Perhaps it is you, and then she slipped into the fog.

I asked a lark that was whispering to its mother about its mother. It approached and said: Perhaps she is you, so please carry me. And it slept in my hand.

I asked myself: Who am I?

The nocturnal echo around me responded: Who am I?

This is I. This is he.

This is all of my imagination.

—Mahmoud Darwish

(TRANSLATED BY SINAN ANTOON)

But expressing emotions, they say, is not one of the attributes of exile.

—Mahmoud Darwish

(TRANSLATED BY SINAN ANTOON)

Copy

adj. Andrajoso, desastrado.
DESANEJARSE. (de des y anejar). r. Trans-
formarse, apartarse de su condición.
DESANGRAMIENTO. m. Acción y efecto de
desangrar o desangrarse.
DESANGRAR. F. Saigner. — It. To bleed. —
A. Ablassen. — It. Dissanguare. — P. Desan-
grar. || tr. Sacar la sangre a una persona o
a un animal, en gran copia. || fig. Agotar
o desaguar un lago, estanque, etc. || fig.
Empobrecer a uno insensiblemente. || —se,
r. Perder mucha sangre; perderla toda.
DESANGRE. m. Colomb. Desangramiento.
DESANIDAR. intr. Dejar las aves el nido.
|| tr. fig. Sacar o echar de un sitio o lugar.
DESANILLAR. (de des y anillar). tr. De-
jar sin anillas aquello que las requiere.

The proactivity, experimentation, and openness that define the field of environ-
mental design are accompanied by a profound sense of respect. This attitude must
guide all of its processes. Through respect for basic forms and certain environ-
ment-shaping principles, both ethics and operational standards are ensured. This
respectful attitude never suppresses creative, innovative forms of proactivity. On
the contrary, such an attitude tends to avoid opportunism and the plunder of
shared goods, resources, and spaces.

It gets fainter and fainter. The capacity for compassion. Life's purpose is the fulfillment of duty, under social pressure. The line of personal responsibility grows fainter and fainter. To escape. To escape responsibility. To escape responsibility through the fulfillment of duty: to submit. You are you, fainter and fainter. To escape compassion copiously.

Behavior only obeys a series of abstractions: it acts in fulfillment of duty. Without personal responsibility. It integrates itself, flees abandonment under social pressure. It doesn't admit fear. It doesn't accept pain. Callously. It denies itself: the central point of pleasure and pain. So faint. It searches openmouthed, like the child you were. It searches as if searching for the maternal site, with its mouth, to obey. Under social pressure, the hook that strengthens and is transformed according to the structure. You're vanishing. Without personal responsibility. The site of the watchtower. The tower, with its hook-mouth. Callously impoverished. To lose one's blood. To lose all of it. In this fog, the fulfillment of duty and responsibility are now a selfsame circumstance. Under laborious construction. The prison of identity. The identity of forty hours a week. To give life, in fulfillment of duty. To take life, in fulfillment of duty. Callously impoverished. Fleeing from pain. Without compassion. You're vanishing. You're a set pinned with the threads of the circumstances: social pressure. There, in the focal point of pleasure and pain, with yourself. You and not you, together. One muzzled and the other submitted, obeying in fulfillment of duty, with yourself. Pleasure and pain, assembling in secret. Under laborious construction. Vanishing.

We've all had this same experience. Pleasure and pain. Distorted. Under social pressure. The pleasure and pain of others. Under social pressure that opens its mouth. That searches in every sense. The force of nature, under social pressure, searching with its mouth. The immediacy of the senses, to communicate. To communicate. To communicate. The focal point with itself. The pleasure and pain of others. The true meaning of the world. Under laborious construction. Since childhood. We've all had this experience, far from our own feeling: to communicate. To open the mouth for the hook to slip in. In this fog where the blood shows through. To lose it. To lose all of it. In fulfillment of duty, because we think it's the same. The ability to see in all that fog: responsibility, the fulfillment of duty. To give or take life. The ability to see the clasp calling out to us in our own tongue, and at which moment, seeping through the fog. Blood. The blood seeping through the fog. To open. To open one's hand and memory: to communicate.

To do is to undo. Copiously. You live because someone cast enough light onto the edge of the highway. The decomposition of light. You live because you removed yourself from your condition while your family prayed, trapped in the fire, undoing darkness and substance. To do is to undo. You live because the soldiers set their march and their checkpoints above the nest. The soldiers plotted a safe shelter with your blood. To lose one's blood, to lose all of it. To lose one's identity. You live, like an animal or like a room ousted from its place. To lose one's place. To lose one's mind. To lose one's address. Because it's precisely this *bird leaving the nest, draining the pond, to be callously impoverished, to be transformed*, that you embraced as you embraced life.

A commonplace: to feel. An order. The decomposition of blood. To lose the edge. To lose the start. To lose one's place. You embraced decomposition as you embraced life. A commonplace: to feel. An order. When you'd cross the checkpoints, you also embraced this *bird leaving the nest*. When they'd interrogate you, you also embraced this *draining*, this *extracting the blood of a person or animal*. Your gaze focused on the lake. You live because the moon touched the stone jutting out of the pond to show you, copiously, its edges. You clung to predation. You clung to opportunism. You clung to proactivity.

To reassemble oneself. Proactivity, opportunism: an order. A tongue, leaving. A gesture, setting sail: a singular place. You're the one who answers the interrogations, the one who stops, identity in hand, at every checkpoint. Copiously. You, not I, are the loser. Copiously. The bad traffic, suspect of the rage spilling out onto the world. You're the one drowning in your own shadow. You live because another five hundred soldiers were tasked with your disappearance. To reassemble oneself. You, not I, are the one who responds: *my chest hides nothing but the dark honey of the one with neither place nor exit.*

The interrogations. You have neither place nor exit. You live. Because others took your disappearance respectfully. You, not I, are the one who'd better stay wide-awake. The image of the prison and its thousand ways of rising up and caving in. The interrogations. Removed from your condition. Designing the environments of your infinite prisons. Opportunism. Proactivity. The sleepless one, monitoring the conditions of respect, because you made yourself disappear. Because you open the shadow of your hand when fear starts to circle. You, not I, live in terror of the weapons and positions. Pursued between the cracks of countries by their very predation.

To lose space. To lose water. To lose place. To lose attitude. To lose respect. To lose proactivity. To lose territory. To lose blood. To lose resources. To lose environments. To lose form. To lose one's way. To lose meaning. To lose one's mind. To lose respect. To lose government. **Copiously. To reassemble oneself.** In curiosity. In heat. **In structure.** In the blood of a person or animal. To lose oneself. To lose all of oneself. All of you, not me. Copiously. You, not me. Abundantly. From a skin of ash. From an ocean of snow. From your shadow's radioactivity. From the territory of burgeoning. To reassemble oneself. With a cutting edge. With ice. With a surgical blow. With hunger.

DESCOMPONIBLE. adj. Susceptible de descomposición.

DESCOMPOSICIÓN. F. Décompositon. — I. Decomposition, Confusion. — A. Zersetzung. — It. Scomposizione. — P. Descomposição. || f. Acción y efecto de descomponer o descomponerse.

DESCOM- POSTURA. (de des y compostura). f. Descomposición. || Desaseo, desaliño. || fig. Descaro, falta de respeto.

Descomposición de la luz

DESCOMPRESIÓN. (de des y compresión). f. Acción de descomprimir.

DESCOMPRIMIR. tr. Dejar libre un cuerpo que se comprime.

DESCOMPUESTAMENTE. adv. m. Con descompostura

DESCOMPUESTO, TA. p. p. irreg. de descomponer. || adj. fig. Inmodesto, atrevido, descortés.

This minimalist design understood the fact that value and wealth are produced at the margins; that is to say, in the far reaches inhabited by the creativity, innovation, and diversity of all societies.

You're vanishing. We've all had the same experience. We think responsibility and the fulfillment of duty are one single thing. Corporate identity. To mold oneself. To consent. Pinned to a set of abstractions. Without a political position. Without a center (pleasure, pain). A person organized according to a principle of power. You and not you will insist on responsible behavior. Obeying the dominant political ideology. To mold oneself. To consent. You're vanishing. Even if the nature of such an orientation is revealed. In all its exteriority. We've all had the same experience. Corporate identity. We align ourselves through the body. Through our color. Through uniformed attire. The style in vogue: to obey. To mold oneself. In all one's exteriority. Such people only change responsibilities and direction along with structure. To be able. To be able to mold oneself. To be able to obey. Corporate identity. We've all had this same experience; we think it's all one single thing. This abrupt phenomenon. The abrupt change at the same time as the changing structure. Structure organizes. To mold oneself. To obey. The structure from the watchtower. You and not you, they watch. They change, abruptly. Without a center. Without a political position. Although their true nature is revealed (pleasure, pain).

You change, abruptly, our concept of identity. Identity and the fulfillment of duty, assembling in secret. You and not you, devoutly. To obey. To mold oneself. As soon as the structure changes. To be able. As soon as the danger changes. To obey. This phenomenon. To give life. To take life. Our usual concept of identity. Clearly the same. There is no authentic self in the present. There isn't. An authentic self in the present. To not be.

To follow, devoutly, the rules of worldly success. Business. Devoutly. Loyalty is identity. To mold oneself. To change loyalties. To change identities. According to the power structure. As soon as it changes. Corporate identity. You and not you, together. Abruptly. Obeying the set of abstractions. To change, clearly. To adjust oneself. To cease to be. To give or take. Life.

To follow the rules of worldly success. You and not you, a walking organism. They are revealed in all their exteriority. To change blood. To change identity. To change loyalties. To obey the new structure. Because, in you, no authentic self is present. To not be. As soon as the danger changes, to deny fear. To deny pain. To deny pleasure (assembling in secret).

To pass the test of adaptability. "Realism." Corporate identity as soon as the danger changes. The ability to obey. As soon as the structure changes. The structure organizes. Copiously. (Pleasure and pain, assembling in secret.) To deny everything. Callously. Even if its true nature is revealed. To jump from one set of responsibilities to another, one set's adaptability to another set's abstractions. To not be. As soon as the danger changes.

In the structure. Hungry. To take the first step. In the water. Fearful. To deliver. The first blow. You. Who have disappeared. Who live. Who launch your thinking from the jungle or from the tunnel. You, not me. In the structure. In pain. **To give.** The first fear. In the leap. Hungry. The first step. Who have disappeared. You. Who live. Who launch the jungle from your thinking or from the tunnel. Facedown. You, not me. Facedown in the water. You, not me. Facedown in fear. You, not me. Facedown in the first blow. You, not me. In the structure.

It's produced in the margins. You are you and your disappointment. The decomposition of the light. Copiously. You and your shadow. You and your setting-free. You are you and your shamelessness, from which you give orders. You and the construction of the tower where you point to me or watch me. It's produced in the margins. The act of decompressing, slovenliness. You are you and the speed at which you shift from one thought to the next. To do is to undo. You and your repetition in someone else's mouth. In the mouth of the society that opens itself to adore you. You are you and your mask. To lose. To lose all of it.

It's produced in the margins. You and your slave-condition. Drowning in its propriety. Drowning in its shadow. Drowning in callous impoverishment. From which you self-modulate each code. You and your hiding place behind the monitor. On the platform. Shameless. Producing your mask. Drowning in its propriety, that is to say. Copiously. Copiously. Just like the petal that peeks a single tip out of the ashes. Just like the laborious construction. Your nubile mouth. Your mouth that opens, drowning callously. Your cadaver-mouth. That is to say.

Observing decomposition isn't an attribute of your circumstances. That is to say. Observing pain isn't an attribute of your circumstances. Say you're displacement. Pilgrimage. Observing the light the tower casts on you isn't an attribute of your circumstances. Say you're the course. The inaccessible nature that pushed stones toward this mountain. Say you're a stone. Let's finish the interrogation.

In sum, the logical/intellectual layer of educational environmental design is focused on defining, with greater or lesser precision, the instructions, the logistics, and the intelligence that permits infrastructure to be used toward the objectives of the educational system. This is the layer that ought to successfully consider, design, and implement tactics and strategies in translating the objectives of the classical educational system within an environment like the Internet.

Lack of human emotions. Reveals. She has a good career: escaping. The career of good impressions. Good impressions: brand-copy-urbanity. What should be felt. To be an expert in what should be felt. Essential point. The fulfillment of duty. A good career: escaping. Without experiencing feeling. Without tension. Without confrontation. Without contradiction. A lack. Copiously. Essential point. To obey, to have to feel. Without empathy. To escape empathic perception. Compassion. If that were the case. That is to say. Empathic perception must disappear. You're vanishing, you and not you, together. You who know very well what one should feel.

You are you and your enemy: a simple person for whom everything is possible. Everything-is-possible becomes the alliance. You are your enemy. Classify that behavior as realistic. Corporate identity. The tower with its hook-mouth. You are the watchtower. The tower that casts light on itself. Classify your own identity: corporate. Without fear. Without pleasure. In fulfillment of duty. You are you and not you: lying beneath the wires, in the tunnels, hiding its true pathology. The absence of yourself. Essential point. The authentic being dragging itself through other circumstances. Underground. Drowned by its own shadow. Copiously. You are you and not you. Without the ability to exist. Shut up in the disguise of efficiency. Corporate identity. To give life. To take life away. In fulfillment of duty. Without fear. Without pleasure. Without pain. A clean cut, surgical, that is to say. A clean cut through one's emotions. Essential point: resistance.

You are you and your resistance. The one that's born of the center. The one that expands the heart. The one that immediately recognizes the conformist's empty soul. You are you and the ability to adjust that light. You are the one who grips that reality by the neck. The tower. That casts light onto the light of your heart. You adjust (corporate identity) to the world's success. Structure organizes. You are you and the structure. You adjust. Perfectly. To every circumstance. You feel gratified, because your heart speaks. To communicate. Your heart that searches with its mouth (pleasure, pain). To communicate. Your newborn heart, drowning in its shadow. You are. What you must be. In fulfillment of duty. You feel. What you must feel. Successful person. You're vanishing. Gratified by your sincerity. The tower that casts light onto your light. Light of watchfulness. You're vanishing. You adjust. That is to say.

It's produced in the margins. You're alive because, as they were killing him, you believed you were overhearing a sexual act. Under laborious construction. You heard the dark moan like an animal's. They were killing him, but you believed and pressed your ear to the wall. A dark moan in contact with the concrete's winter. Under laborious construction. You're alive because they were killing him but you, you silently rested your hand against the cold, and, charged with sensuality, every blow stopped you still and took your breath away.

You, not I, are produced in the margins. It has a passport to anywhere on earth. You, not I, carry your identity document. You live: you give orders to the forces of human nature. You believe in the worship of army boots. You too come with me. Underground. You too sink. You too take root. You too scatter seeds of watchfulness that burgeon into webs and cables. You, not I, have been disappeared by your own extermination. We're going to bloom. To rise. To reassemble oneself.

The extreme space is what produces creativity. I don't have any. Creativity. I don't live in the present. I don't sense anything but lies in blood's presence. She, not you, sprawled facedown on the pavement. It's not creative. It's a brilliant color. A shattering. Extreme space. Its mouth encountering the little pebbles on the highway. You live inside the heavy bubble where time doesn't pass. You live because someone appeared to tell you they were killing you. In another reality.

Uncommonly large, enormous. We've all had this experi-
ence. The decomposition of blood. The decomposition of
light. You're vanishing. Say you're a stone and we'll finish
with this excavation. Say you're a stone and we'll finish with
these circumstances. There's no other option. You answered.
I'm the inventor of fear when it proves necessary. We want
proof of your identity. *Very far from the ordinary. I am. The
inventor of fear.*

Uncommonly large. I'm the inventor of fear. Without pleasure. Without pain. I'm a stone. Finish this excavation. I'm the tower with the hook-mouth. I'm the nature, in sum, that points toward definition. Nature's open mouth. Finish your interrogation. I'm the inventor. To be able to think. In fulfillment of duty. Finish it. We've all had this same experience.

It isn't an attribute. Here. It isn't an attribute of your circumstances. Repeat after me. It isn't an attribute of your circumstances. The interrogation. Repeat. That you slipped into the dark volume of this water in hopes of hiding there. Repeat. That **fear** betrayed you. Repeat. The only attribute of my circumstances is the light from the tower. Repeat. The only attribute of my circumstances involves betrayal.

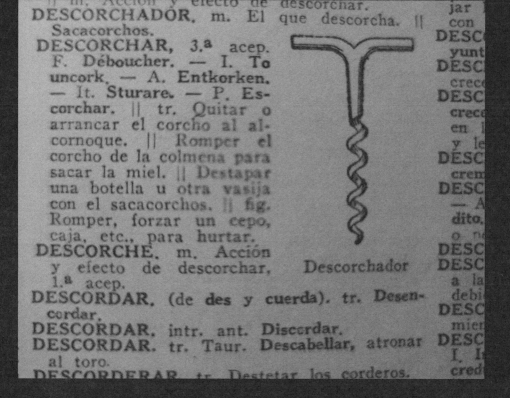

Descorchador

Finally, the portable computer, a material good, will become a public good if donated by a company, civil society organization, or one of the establishment's own collaborators for all the students of an establishment, community, or nation. The administration will determine whether the good, be it material or public in nature, has or does not have a tragic destiny.

The spectacle of consciousness. A person who produces artificial feelings. Without shame, without pain, without self-pity. Property in fulfillment of duty. Reversible identity. It dramatizes the role of the idea: consciousness dictated by the power structure. In all its exteriority. Derived. Because people are actually highly unpredictable. People are actually highly dependent, suggestive, and ready to obey. People are highly feminine. Reversible identity. You and not you: people. To not be. You're vanishing. Derived in its contradiction. In fulfillment of duty. You clearly reflect your identity. You surrender, like a woman. You let the boot of structure advance over your thinking, scornfully: to not be.

Scornfully. To be, in the feminine. With scorn for yourself. Not to be. Without access to your interior. Without self-consciousness. Surrendered in repetition. With your empty hand. With your hand empty of responsibility. Reversible. Hating yourself. Not understanding. Lacking in genuine emotions. To be, in the feminine. Scornfully. *"Gentlemen, I'm going to ask you to rid yourselves of your sense of pity. We must annihilate them ... everywhere, wherever they may be found."* Structure orders. Copiously. Structure speaks through its apparatus of phonation. Didn't you know? To be, in the feminine. You struggle to understand yourself. *I struggle to understand myself.* You spoke your first truth. Stripped of itself, it obeyed. Structure orders. As soon as structure took a turn, scornfully (to be, in the feminine), that person is unable to understand. You and not you are a prior being. Prior: the place from which understanding is pursued. You and not you are still confronted with your prior emptiness. Scornfully. You and not you are a woman who will be unable to. Do nothing but open the mouth containing the persistent emptiness: a tower. The watchtower. That casts light onto your light to corner suffering, your center (pleasure, pain). The tower with its hook-mouth. Without confrontation. Submissively.

Submissively: a characteristic that separates you from the others. Basic constellation. A set of responsibilities to escape. To escape. To escape. Surrendering. To be, in the feminine. To escape one's own identity. To be, scornfully. A set of new responsibilities. A characteristic that separates you from the others. No one knows. No one is aware of it. The others: you and not you. Derived. The resulting identity: betrayal. To escape. Intensifying hatred toward oneself. Scornfully. Feminine, woman. Intensifying emptiness toward itself. Scornfully. A basic constellation. *I struggle to understand myself.*

Nature. This inner emptiness. It tends to escape others' perception. Because you know how to manipulate your behavior. To mold oneself. In fulfillment of duty. Expert in appearances. You're vanishing. Without tension between what is and what should be. Tension is a sickness. To mold oneself. In fulfillment of duty. As often as ordered by structure.

At last, the good. This is you. Take me with you. This is you. This is me. Take me to you. Copiously. Someone cast light onto the edge of the highway. This is you. This is me. The decomposition of light illuminated your shattered mouth. The portable computer. You. At last. I. Breaking the cork in the beehive to remove the honey. Under laborious construction. At last. Life.

They shattered your mouth and shattered the lock. **At last, the good.** This you is me. At last. A tragic destiny at the edge of the highway. Say you're a stone. Materially. The decomposition of light illuminated you facedown. This you is me. A tragic destiny in front of the watchtower. Say the army boots dragged you here. Commonly, the good. This you is me. The volume of water and its shadow.

And I, it comes with me. Uncorked, uprooted from itself. **This you is me.** Climbing the tower with its hook-mouth. Gagged. To be able to think: this you is me. This you transported from a tragic destiny. Displacement. Say you're a stone. Let's finish the interrogation. This you is me. This is you. From the violated lock of your own language. To uproot. The tongue, the mouth, the structure. Completely material. Donated by the collaborator of the establishment. Unseeing. You're coming up with me. Say it. You're coming up with me.

Under laborious construction. **A tragic destiny.** Common. Copiously. This is you. Portable. You're alive. Every code. This is you. You're coming with me. You're coming to bloom. Petal-tip beneath the ash.

Uprooted by the circumstances. **Repetition.** An attribute. Say you gradually made your way into the shelter of this water. An attribute of your circumstances. Say it suits you. That you washed the pain as you controlled your breath. Say this is your gunpowder. This is your fascination with reality. Say you saw the shattered mouth against the highway and the image blooming lusciously betrayed you. The spectacle of consciousness: an attribute. Let's finish the investigation.

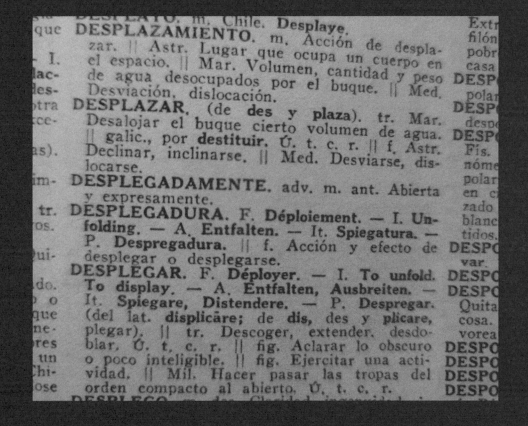

However, under no circumstances does the material format of an intellectual work change the nature of the good that remains, in one way or another, intellectual.

You are him and you are you. Reversible. Prior. Unable to understand. A responsible individual. In all its exteriority. To surrender requires one to rethink. To hate oneself. Resulting identity. Derived. Corporate identity. To surrender in such a way. External identity. Inauthentically. To surrender. You are him and you are you. The watchtower. The nature of your inner emptiness. In all its exteriority. You ask permission. To surrender. The concept of identity. You ask permission. Your mouth seeks a guard. You look for the hook-mouth of the tower that casts permission to continue. *Can I do it now?* The nature of your inner emptiness. *Can I do it now?* Permission to continue. You're vanishing. Permission to continue. You're empty. You simulate the sense of surrender. You are you and your extermination. Derived from the change in structure. The last perversion of our times. In all its exteriority. Emptiness gives the appearance of feeling.

To hate oneself. To give the appearance of feeling. The result of surrender. To betray oneself constantly. To hate oneself more the greater the surrender. To not be. The mouth seeks the world's success. "Realism." To not be is merely the result. Classify this behavior: identity, strengthened. To forget. To search fruitlessly, with the mouth, the fulfillment of duty. Inauthentically. Without confrontation. To hate oneself. Searching for an ideology of duty. To be prior in the face of its own emptiness. Searching. Fruitlessly. Able to derive, criminally. Criminally: the emptiness gives the appearance of feeling. It breaks social laws. Although a lesser variation does exist. Criminally: committing injustices disguised as legality. The emptiness gives the appearance of feeling. Criminally. You are him and you are you. Reversible. Realism. Derived. It internalizes its power. It violates. Openly. It hates love. It hates the root of its development. It hates the opposition to its idealization. Empty. It rejects the dominant writing. You're vanishing. Classify this behavior: an identity that hides, criminally. Disguised with legality. Classify this behavior: in search of an authoritarian identity. Mouth in search of an authority. To be bloodthirsty and to be itself, in secret, assembling. Easy to hate oneself if hate is located in an external object. To hate oneself. In all its exteriority. The world's success. Mask of virtue. Mask of greatness. To hate oneself like a god. It's easy. Classify this behavior: identity based on obedience. Without personal responsibility. You're vanishing. There's no escape for resentment.

To recover unbearable incompetence. To not be. Without hope. To find a key. To hate oneself. The identification with power. You are you and the one who grips you by the neck. Unbearable competence. The key of the one who hates oneself. You are you and the one who opens their hand to liberate you. The world's success. Ambition searching with its mouth.

Classify this behavior: _____

Observing **space** isn't an attribute of your circumstances. Say you're a stone. Dragged all the way here by military boots. Let's finish the excavation. Observing the place occupied by a body in space isn't an attribute of your circumstances. Say the blood that appeared on your hands was part of the water. Observing motion isn't an attribute of your circumstances. Close your eyes. Close your eyes. To observe repetition isn't...

Place occupied by a body in space. To displace. The intellect. You're vanishing. Under no circumstances. You are me and you are you: place, which occupies a body. A change in nature. The center (pleasure), pain. The spectacle of consciousness. Take me to the displacement on the highway. Take me to you. Take me with you.

Place occupied by a body. In space. Place occupied by a body. You are. You, and not you. Place shifted by velocity. In space. A walking platform. Under no circumstances does it change, the good. Volume, quantity. You, and not you. In its displacement. The decomposition of light. You cross the sky until you reach the highway. Intellectual. Unchanging.

Place occupied: I've already said. I've already said body. I've already switched the troops from a compact order to an open order. I've already said a walking platform. Take me. I've already said I have a stone's identity. Take me with you.

Volume of water. To obey. Displaced. Volume and weight of water. I've already said I'm a stone. Under no circumstances does it change, the good. I've already said I was dragged to the highway. Volume of water reflecting space. Take me. Clarity uncloaked in the expression of something. To unfold. To extend. A platform being deviated. Unwillingly. Water. The good remains the good.

Deshacer los montones.

DESAMOR. F. Désamour. — I. Disregard, Desaffection, Enmity. — A. Tsneignag.—It. Disamore, Odio. — P. Desamor. (de des y amor). || m. Mala correspondencia al afecto de uno. || Falta del sentimiento y afecto que inspiran ciertas cosas. || Enemistad, aborrecimiento.

DESAMORADAMENTE. adv. m. Sin amor ni afecto; con esquivez.

DESAMORADO, DA. p. p. de desamorar. || adj. Que no tiene amor o no lo manifiesta.

DESAMORAR. tr. Hacer perder el amor. Ú. t. c. r.

DESAMOROSO, SA. adj. Que no tiene amor o agrado.

DESAMORRAR. (de des y amorrar). tr. fam. Hacer que uno levante la cabeza o rompa el silencio.

The concept of the peer [or peers] indicates an association in which a person or thing symmetrically corresponds to another in a relationship of equality.

Reversible identity. It's not only the result of the self's redemption. Installed, the surface acts continually: the conformist's empty soul. Under lock and key. Social pressure and empty soul. They continually strengthen each other under lock and key. Facing what must be faced. Obeying the structure. Reversible identity. Under lock and key: to hate oneself more. To loathe. To hate perfection, in the feminine. The exchange. To want love in exchange for power. That buzz. To love in exchange for power. To love perfection: reversible. Perfection, in the feminine. It isn't only simplicity or shortage. The lack of being. But rather labor, shoulder to shoulder, in the capacity of changing abruptly. To abruptly change identities. Reversible. To reassemble oneself. To destroy. To destroy an identity. To construct another identity. Abruptly. To destroy. For love. In exchange for power. An identity can be devoured by charitable activities, and, simultaneously, live full of hatred. Hating obedience. Hating solely to feel power in the face of submission. The submissive one who hates, under lock and key, obedience. The conformist's empty soul.

You're vanishing. There's a problem with obedience. To destroy oneself and reassemble oneself yields, after all, some consequence or other. A dark side unceasing. A dark side aggrandized by power.

We've all had this experience: to want love. We've all received love in exchange for power, since childhood. You're vanishing. You hate asking for permission. *Can I do it now?* You hate. Love is without confrontation. Love is to stop in your tracks before your emptiness. Without pleasure. Without pain. Inauthentically: a mask incapable of feeling. Mother of simulation. Love and power aren't the same thing. Responsibility and the fulfillment of duty aren't the same thing. Are you vanishing? To reassemble oneself. You have no place or exit. You search for a key. To overtake. Without fear. Without pain. You try to get your shoe to advance across what you find insufferable. You try to get your shoe to advance across yourself. To destroy oneself. To reassemble oneself. Constantly. The identification with the very hand that grips your neck, princess. That makes you kneel down, life. Participating in power.

Success can also set you free. Ambition. A career. An education. To give a good impression in exchange for power. Copy-brand-urbanity. The world's success.

It's reciprocated. **A relationship of equality.** Expressing emotions isn't an attribute of your circumstances. Lack of feeling. To express. To cause to lose. A relationship of equality. The place isn't the trap. The trap is to repeat oneself. The place isn't the trap. The trap is to repeat oneself. Losing isn't an attribute of your circumstances.

Enormous. Sovereign. Above god. That means sleeping. To live without the pain of life. Without pleasure. Above god. This is the layer that should be thought about. Enormous. Above god. Outside of time. What have you done today? Say you're a stone. That the army boots flung you all the way here. That the blood you carry was from the mouth that shattered on the highway. What have you done today? You slept.

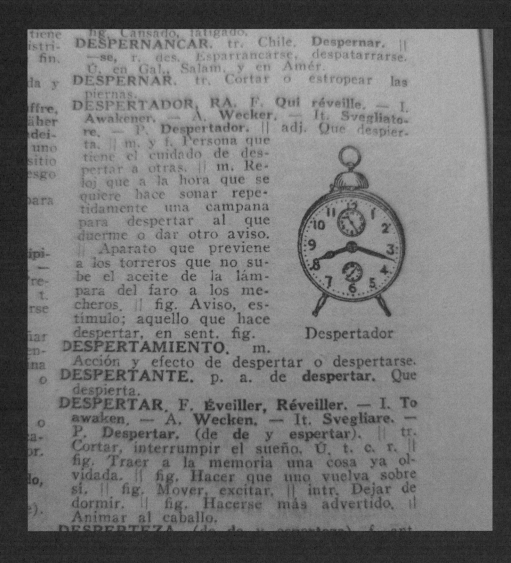

This phase focuses on the search for solutions that stimulate creativity, favor innovation, and prevent the cessation, privatization, and enclosure of intellectual goods that constitute the shared patrimony of societies on the global level.

As long as the structure remains intact, it retains its value and hatred need not be projected. When the structure collapses, when impossible promises are made, when part of power is lost, hatred will come to the surface. To hate others who want love in exchange for power. The world's success. Love in exchange for power. The fulfillment of duty. Reversible. Another incapacity: to experience grief for life, to experience grief for destruction. What will you do now amid the collapse of the structure? It burgeons in you. A wound burgeons in you. The open wound. How to experience grief in the lack of authenticity? Your personality is the lie about love. Are you vanishing?

Humanity should have spared itself such horror. Your pathology, under lock and key, enclosed in fulfillment of duty. The self incapable of feeling. The self without being. Humanity should have spared itself such horror.

Welcome to the path of your psychosis. Welcome to the path of confrontation. Welcome to the path of your pain. Welcome to your cowardice. Any other path lacks hope. To reassemble oneself. In your counterpart.

One constructs time. In this phase, solutions are sought. An attribute of your circumstances. One constructs time. To exhaust. To lose. To change. To resignify. To repeat. One constructs time. To hate oneself like a God. One constructs the circumstances. Say you're a cloud.

The emptiness gives the impression of feeling. Say you're a cloud displaced across this resignification. One constructs time. Say that during your displacement you found the place to brand and jot things down. To manifest oneself. One constructs one's own significance. Say you're the weight and the density.

Celestial **displacement.** Signification. The place that occupies the emptiness of this hatred. To hate oneself like **a God.** Mask of virtue. Mask of greatness. A god. With the gentleness of honey. To burgeon. To transform. To displace. To occupy the body of emptiness. The decomposition of light. Pleasure. Center.

Classify this behavior: _____

Classify this perception: _____

Classify this signified: _____

Person tasked with awakening others. You've never been you. In this phase, solutions are sought. Avoid closing. Avoid breathing. Copiously, you'll see. You've never been you. That is to say. Shared patrimony of societies. To inherit. To resignify. To contain. Open the light of what seems to be your hand. Open the light of what seems to be your vision. Open the contact of what seems to be a mouth. To disappear. To dislocate. To uproot. The emptiness of the impression of feeling. To feel life. To feel pain. To feel pleasure. Derived.

Ringing repeatedly to awaken. The light of what seems to be your hand joins the light of what seems to be a flame. A fire that splits, like a God. To hate oneself. You've never been you. A dislocation dissolving, global. You've never been either fear or circumstances. That stimulate creativity. You haven't been *from the missing point of the animal I am.* To signify.

Not being acquires another significance. Stripped of identity, it acquires another significance. Empty, it acquires another significance. Under certain circumstances. To be global means to not be. Under certain circumstances. A copy of everything. The one tasked with awakening. The cloud. The flower. The animal. The circumstance. The stone thrown into the street. The darkness. Copiously. **A copy of everything invisible.** A copy of everything displaced. One constructs time. The abundant place. Singular.

Identification with power acquires another significance. To reassemble oneself. Like a God. According to the circumstances. **To occupy a place in the body of water.** Like a God. To occupy a place in the body of the sky. To occupy a place in the body of magnetism. Identification with power acquires another significance. To reassemble oneself. In sync with the circumstances. To occupy a place in the vegetal beat of the desert. Displacement. To occupy a place in the hot silence of sand. Like a God, it acquires another significance. Identification with power. Acquires another circumstance.

Let's finish the interrogation. This isn't an army. It's a forest. Let's finish the interrogation. This isn't an army. It's a flock. Let's finish the interrogation. This isn't an army. It's an ocean of blood.

COPIA. F. Abondance, Copie. — I. Copious-
ness, Abundance, Copy, Transcript. — A.
Ueberfluss, Kopie. — It. y P. Copia, (del
lat. copia). f. Abundancia de una cosa,
|| Traslado o reproducción de un escri-
to. || En los tratados de sintaxis, lista de
nombres y verbos, con los casos que rigen.
|| Escrito o papel de música, en que pun-
tualmente se pone el contenido de otro es-
crito o papel, impreso o manuscrito. || Obra
de pintura, de escultura o de otro género,
que se ejecuta reproduciendo otra obra aná-
loga con entera igualdad. || Imitación servil
del estilo o de las obras de escritores o ar-
tistas. || Imitación o remedo de una persona.
|| **Retrato.** || Razón que la contaduría de la
catedral daba por escrito a cada partícipe en
diezmos, de lo que había de percibir de una
cilla o dezmatorio. || Razón que tomaba de
la misma contaduría el arrendador de los
diezmos para saber lo que había de dar a
cada partícipe. || Poét. Pareja.

*The means of collaborative production proposed by the Internet is not based on
the acritical copy of shared/free existing intellectual goods, but rather in the de-
termination to employ what others have produced, what belongs to each person
due to their human condition, to each community as cultural heritage, toward ad-
vancing the production and experience of new shared intellectual goods [equally
or more creative than their inherited originals]. This is the future form of produc-
tion: an age-old collaborative form that defines humans, a profound form that
produces other works that cannot possibly be produced individually.*

To interrupt sleep. To make someone come to their senses.

Bibliography

Agamben, Giorgio. *La comunidad que viene.* (*La communità che viene*, 1990.) Translated by José Luis Villacañas, Claudio La Rocca, and Ester Quirós. Valencia, Spain: Editorial Pre-Textos, 1996.

Aronson, Eric, and Shelly Rosenbloom. "Space Perception in Early Infancy: Perception within a Common Auditory-Visual Space." *Science* 172 (June 11, 1971).

Darwish, Mahmoud. *In the Presence of Absence.* (*Fī Ḥaḍrat al-Ghiyāb*, 2006.) Translated by Sinan Antoon. Brooklyn: Archipelago Books, 2011.

Diccionario hispánico universal: Enciclopedia ilustrada en lengua española. Mexico City: W. M. Jackson Editores, 1956.

Ekelöf, Gunnar. *Poemas.* Translated by Franciso J. Uriz. Barcelona: Plaza & Janés, 1981.

Gelb, Barbara, and Arthur Gelb. *O'Neill*, 870. New York: Harper & Row, 1973 (revised).

Gombrowicz, Witold. *Ferdydurke* (1937). Translated by Virgilio Piñera and Humberto Rodríguez Tomeu. Barcelona: Seix Barral, 2001. Translation first published 1947 by Argos (Buenos Aires).

Gruen, Arno. *The Insanity of Normality: Toward Understanding Human Destructiveness.* (*Der Wahnsinn der Normalität. Realismus als Krankheit*, 1987.) Translated by Hildegarde Hannum and Hunter Hannum. Berkeley: Human Development Books, 2007. Translation first published 1992 by Grove Weidenfeld (New York).

Manvell, Roger, and Heinrich Fraenkel. *The Incomparable Crime.* New York: G. P. Putnam's Sons, 1967.

Mitscherlich, Alexander, and Margarete Mitscherlich. *The Inability to Mourn: Principles of Collective Behavior.* (*Die Unfähigkeit zu trauern*, 1967.) Translated by Beverley R. Placzek. New York: Grove Press, 1975.

Rulfo, Juan. *Pedro Páramo* (1955). Mexico City: Secretaría de Educación Pública, Colección Lecturas Mexicanas, 1984.

FOR THE EPIGRAPHS THAT PRECEDE EVERY CHAPTER

Vercelli, Ariel. "Aprender la Libertad: El diseño del entorno educativo y la producción colaborativa de los contenidos básicos comunes." The author's blog. Buenos Aires, January 2006. www.ariel vercelli.org/all.pdf. Translated by Robin Myers.

Acknowledgments

A brief selection from this book appeared in *Plumwood Mountain*. Another selection was published as a booklet accompanying the activities of Poetry International Rotterdam, where, in 2018, Dorantes was one of the festival's resident poets.